To

_____

From

_____

Date

_____

Marriage
Is a
Balance Beam

Marriage

Is a
Balance Beam

Carole D. Bos

Baker Books

A Division of Baker Book House Co
Grand Rapids, Michigan 49516

© 1997 by Carole D. Bos

Published by Baker Books
a division of Baker Book House Company
P.O. Box 6287, Grand Rapids, MI 49516-6287

Printed in the United States of America

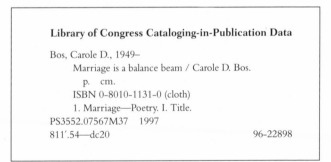

Library of Congress Cataloging-in-Publication Data

Bos, Carole D., 1949–
    Marriage is a balance beam / Carole D. Bos.
      p.   cm.
    ISBN 0-8010-1131-0 (cloth)
    1. Marriage—Poetry. I. Title.
PS3552.07567M37   1997
811'.54—dc20   96-22898

To my husband
James Bos
My lover
My companion
My best friend

Contents

Contents

Preface

*W*hen I was a little girl, I used to dream about "getting married." My favorite toy was a beautiful bride doll my parents gave me for Christmas when I was eight years old. I still have the doll.

Today, when I reflect on that dream, I know the truth. What I really dreamed about was being a bride. What I really planned for was having a wedding.

When I was a teenager, I bought bridal magazines so I could look at all the beautiful bridal gowns. Before I even had a fiancé, I dreamed about how I would look in a wedding dress. I thought how wonderful it would be to look like—and be—a princess for a day. I was in love with the idea of a wedding before I was in love with the man I would marry.

Despite all the dreams I had about my wedding, I never really gave much thought to marriage. Even after Jim and I were engaged, I never thought marriage would be something to work at. I never believed we would disagree about anything significant.

I learned, over the years, that marriage is a balance beam. It is as easy for an unsuspecting marriage partner to fall off the beam as it is difficult for an

11

untrained gymnast to attempt a gold-medal performance.
The poems in this book reflect my growth from an un-
trained novice to a member of an Olympic-team marriage.

As a new bride, I believed nothing was difficult as long
as "we are together." Very early, however, I realized I had
idealistic expectations about marriage. Although I had good
role models with strong marriages, I was not sure how to
make my own marriage strong. I started to ask different
questions. I began to understand that each marriage is
unique. I discovered, eventually, that the unknowable as-
pects of marriage contribute to its strength. I found out
those same unknowable elements can cause uncertainty
and fear. I had to learn to trust my husband and my mar-
riage. I also had to learn to trust and follow my own
instincts.

This book is, therefore, a celebration of the joys and sor-
rows of marriage. My poems honor the process of forging
a union that sustains and strengthens both partners. My re-
flections acknowledge that combining two different lives
is an arduous, but worthwhile, undertaking.

Acknowledgments

*F*ifty percent of all marriages fail. Today's laws make it easy to end a difficult marriage. The problem is: All marriages have difficulties. All marriages require hard work and constant sacrifice, especially at the beginning. Sometimes it is easier to give up than to try. Sometimes it is less painful to leave than to stay. Sometimes staying is not a viable option.

I learned about marriage from watching my parents. My parents learned about marriage from watching my grandparents. I was raised in a loving home, but my parents, like all marriage partners, had disagreements. I observed how they worked through their problems. I learned what makes a marriage strong. Not until I was married, facing similar issues, did I understand how complicated marriage really is.

Jim and I have been blessed with a great marriage, but we have had to work at it. After twenty-eight years, we have learned how to compromise. We have learned how to support each other. We now understand that putting the interests of each other first benefits both. We have learned, but sometimes we forget the lessons. This book is about learning and forgetting marriage lessons.

13

Acknowl-
edgments

I want to acknowledge my parents, James and Alberdean Berkenpas. They showed me how a loving marriage can sustain and strengthen marriage partners. Thank you for being such good role models.

My husband is my best and closest friend. Together we have forged a marriage that gives us both support and loving encouragement. Providing solace from a demanding professional life, our home is the place I long for when I am away. Jim is the person I most want to be with no matter where I am. This book is a celebration of the joy and contentment that results from a solid marriage. Thank you, Jim, for being who you are.

My editor, Betty DeVries, must take significant credit for this book. More than anyone else, she has prodded me to be the best writer I can be. Thank you, Betty, for your honest opinions. Thank you for your wisdom.

I am grateful, most of all, to God who has blessed me with a marriage that gives me tremendous personal fulfillment.

Unknowable

We didn't know
  Marriage is like
Combining two chemicals
  For the first time:
The actual reaction
  Is largely unknowable
Until the formula is mixed
  In the beaker.

I knew your character
  Beforehand
While you were still
  Unattached

Unknowable

I did not expect
   Profound changes
Once our lives were merged
   In the marriage beaker.

When two chemicals are blended
   For the first time
Scientists experiment
   With the outcome:
Will the molecules
   Combine?
   Explode?
   Separate?

Our marriage has been
   A permanent experiment:
Once the first two chemicals combined
   Without separation
   Without explosion
We have consistently added
   More unknown molecules
   More untested combinations.

The result
   Is a unique solution
That may have separated
   Or exploded
In a different beaker.

After decades of adding
   New mixtures
We have learned
   What only experience can teach:
Marriage is
   Unknowable at the start
   Inscrutable along the way
   Unique unto itself.

What a great formula
   For combining two lives!

This Day

"From this day forward"
A commitment for life
A day of excitement
We've become "man and wife."

The day of the wedding
"Our Day" with its frills
Follows a frenzy
Of planning and bills.

Sublime admiration
Joy and delight
At the moment of vows
Optimism burns bright.

The best of intentions
Motivate the "I do"
But immeasurable efforts
Make marriage ring true.

Will we have courage
To look past our faults
That will soon come to light
At the end of the waltz?

Will we have patience
Understanding and care
If plans are disrupted
If we both face despair?

Reality is not
What we want it to be
Can we focus on "us"
And sublimate "me"?

This Day

Our singular effort
Commanding our best
Is to make THIS DAY each day
We'll give that goal no rest.

The beauty of marriage,
Like a true work of art,
Is the process of crafting
With THIS DAY a mere start.

Blueprints

Building a marriage
Is like building a house;
The question is:
Who drew the blueprint?

For us
Years of experience have drawn
A reliable blueprint
For sensible living.

I wish I could read blueprints!

Marriage Wells

Marriage is a well
Capable of producing
  Potable or
  Polluted water

Potable water
  sustains
Polluted water
  destroys

From our marriage well
We can draw

Enduring stability
Disruptive adversity

Peaceful harmony
Warring discord

Life-enhancing freedom
Restrictive control

Loving encouragement
Belittling criticism

Nurturing intercourse
Disrespectful abuse

Peace of mind
Constant fear

Thank you, Lord,
For giving us a well
  Unpolluted
Free from
  Rotting debris
  Putrescent garbage

Thank you
For potable water
  Satisfying desires
  Sustaining our lives.

Keys to Compromise

In the beginning
I thought I made
   Heroic compromises;
I dwelled too much
   On the "hero" part.

Establishing our home
I thought I should teach
   Countless lessons;
I dwelled too much
   On the "teaching" role.

During early disagreements
I thought I gave in
  Unnecessarily;
I dwelled too much
  On the "I" word.

I saw a multitude
  Of faults:
I thought I needed
  To correct his
  Not mine
Until
I found the greatest fault
  In me:
Trying to change him
  Instead of myself.

Concerns are different now:

Does the issue really matter?
  If the answer is "no"
What is the point?

What am I giving up?
  If the answer is "nothing"
Why should I care?

Can I adjust my thinking?
  If the answer is "yes"
Why waste time arguing?

We have learned to
  Listen first
  Think next
  Speak last
  Teach by example

We have found
  Our keys to compromise.

If only
  I didn't
Keep losing
  Those keys!

Rule Exceptions

Blackened lungs
from
Smoky haze

Yellowed teeth
from
Inhaled pollution

Reddened throat
from
Willful irritation

Cigarettes
A major discord

He smoked
  I rebelled.

I promised
  Not to nag
  Initially
I failed
  Instantly

He promised
  To quit
  Half-heartedly
He failed
  Intentionally

I banned all cigarettes
  From the bedroom
Especially
  After passionate moments.
Neither of us
  Understood
The other's needs.

Finally
　After seven years
He quit
　Completely.

Improbable
But easier
　He said
Than resisting
A daily barrage
　Of complaints.

We had found
　An exception
To the rule
　Against nagging.

A Loose Wire

I heard your comments
But the static was loud
We must have
A loose wire someplace.

You heard my call
But noise interfered
The line must have
A loose wire someplace.

The room is quiet
We stand face-to-face
Your message is lost
The loose wire is in me.

Untouchable Jugular

The unthinkable happened to my friend
  A judge.
Her husband
  Walked into her chambers
  And shot her.

He knew where she was vulnerable:
  In the jugular.
Within minutes after the fatal shot
  She was dead
  Bled to death in her courtroom.

A physical insult to the jugular
  Ends a life
  Like my friend's

But an emotional assault
　　Blows a life apart.

I define "going for the jugular" as
　　A cruel intent to harm:
Within minutes fatal words
　　Mortally wound a relationship
　　Bleed it dry of love
Treasonous exploits
　　Lacerate a union
　　Sever conjoined commitments.

To make our marriage work
We have vowed
Our jugulars
　　Are untouchable

　　Destructive words
　　Vicious actions
Are
　　Off-limits
　　Even if truth is at issue.

Physical insults
  May not end life
Mental assaults
  May not shatter a relationship
But a carefully directed aim
  At a penetrable jugular
Produces fatal consequences
  To body and mind.

I reject the premise
That partners
  In a caring relationship
Could "go for the jugular."

I don't believe
Loving partners
  Could allow poison
To remain undisguised at the tip
  Of a knife.

Excuses abound:
  "I wanted to teach a lesson"

Untouchable
Jugular

As though forcing a spouse
   Through manipulation
Justifies the strong-arm approach.
I think honest differences
   Lead to growth.

"Look what you made me do"
As though a victim
   Is responsible
For inappropriate behavior.
I think self-control
   Needs revitalizing.

"We're totally honest with each other"
As though feigned innocence
   Is a genuine cover
For malicious words.
Alibis are irrelevant
   For on-target missiles.

"I didn't mean it"
As though the result
   Of hurtful words
Is ever unexpected or unintended.

The excuses are not credible.
After those excuses failed
    We both agreed:
The jugular is off-limits
    To unvarnished candor
    To empty excuses
    To lethal actions.

I wish our method
    Could have worked for my friend.
On that fatal day
    She didn't have
        a chance.

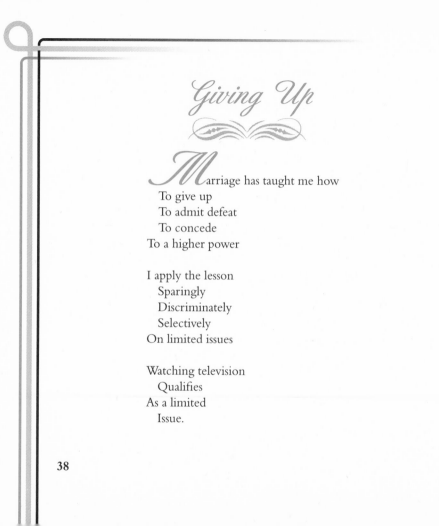

Giving Up

Marriage has taught me how
  To give up
  To admit defeat
  To concede
To a higher power

I apply the lesson
  Sparingly
  Discriminately
  Selectively
On limited issues

Watching television
  Qualifies
As a limited
  Issue.

I need
    Unparalleled patience
    Unlimited tolerance
To make it through
    The late news.

He needs
Unparalleled control
    Of the remote
Unlimited access
    To every available channel.

Asleep,
    Remote control in hand,
He knows
When I switch
    Channels

Matchless hearing
    Sightless vision
Awaken him
    Every time.

Giving Up

I recognize
   And accept
Lost battles
   These days

I don't mind.

Better
   To give up
When I don't
   Care
And use my banked
   Concessions
When I do.

Mere Words

I only meant
  To question
  Not to harm
I razed the toll-free bridge
  Connecting mutual trust

I should have
  Asked you
  Privately
Sustaining courage left me
  While we were on our own.

Now the gap between us
  Is not closed
  By an embrace

My arms, my soul
  Are empty, missing you

Brash, I am alone
   Isolated by a distance
   I created
Not with Mere Words
   With public accusations.

You know me well
   You listened
   Not just heard
You understood the meaning
   Of my hidden thoughts

How can I end
   This unforced loneliness?
   Mere Words
Will not revive
   The trust we shared so long

Mere Words
   Will not repair
   The damage
I have caused
   To you, to us

Mere Words
  Will not rebuild
  The solid structure
I destroyed
  With callous whim

Mere Words
  Will not return
  Free passage
On our bridge
  Restored by human faults.

Home Remedies

*O*ur quiet talks are like sleep
A time for the body to heal itself

Our solitude is like rest
A time for the soul to strengthen itself

Our intimacy is like stretching
A time for our love to expand itself

Clouds

Marriage problems
Are cloud formations
With a twist:
We,
Not nature,
Determine the extent of
The haze
The gloom
The rainbow.

But
As clouds
Make a sunset
Arresting
Memorable

Clouds

So difficulties
Can make marriage
Stimulating
Resilient.

Whether life's nebulae
Are enveloping mists
Or luminous horizons
Depends on
Our attitude
Our endurance
Our fortitude.

The trouble is
We don't have
Nature's competence!

The Last Word

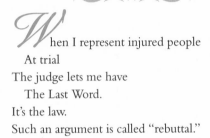

When I represent injured people
 At trial
The judge lets me have
 The Last Word.
It's the law.
Such an argument is called "rebuttal."

When I represent myself
 In a marriage dispute
I must fight the impulse
 To have the Last Word.
It's counterproductive.
Such an argument is called "waste of time."

The Last Word

I have two hurdles to overcome
When I disagree at home:
  My human nature;
  My training as a cross examiner.
Both push me, inevitably,
  Toward the Last Word.

On technical grounds
I wouldn't lose many arguments:
  I'm a trained advocate.
On human grounds
I wouldn't win many disagreements
  If I behaved like an advocate at home.

What's the point
  Of having the Last Word?
It makes me feel better—
  I think I've won.
It gives me satisfaction—
  I think he's lost.

When I've won an argument at home
    I rarely feel good
It's not like winning in court.
To me, a fair compromise
    Is a true win at home
A result that makes us both proud.

Giving up the Last Word in marriage
    Is against human nature
It's hard for me to swallow
    That last sentence.
But getting to the First Word
    Of a just compromise
Is worth the concession.

Evening Musicals

During the night
My husband
Plays percussion instruments
Loudly

He uses the full range
Slowly, initially
Gaining momentum
As snares give way to timpani

Fortunately, mercifully
The music stops
When he sleeps
Soundly

Tchaikovsky's "1812 Overture"
Has found a great performer:
Cymbals clashing, kettle drums vibrating
My husband's audience is powerless
Totally

One last crescendo
Then silence
Until another evening musical
Tomorrow night.

He says I sometimes play
The tuba
During practice sessions
I don't believe him.

He doesn't believe me
Unless he awakens
Hoarse
The next morning.

Evening
Musicals

Grinning, he clears his throat
And stores his instruments
For daytime repose.
Sheepishly: Did I snore last night?
No, honey—
You just played Tchaikovsky.

Tears

Black wall
Tapered at the
  Ends
White letters
Spelling names of
  Friends

Lost lives
Crushed spirits
  All
Vietnam
Our generation's
  War.

53

Tears

You volunteered
For rain-swept
  Land
I cried
And failed to
  Understand

Why fight
This war—it isn't
  Ours
Why risk
Your life—it now is
  Mine.

Orders spared you
From the jungle
  War
You did not face
The strife, monsoons and
  Gore.

We stand now
At this wall of
  Pain

Its blackness
Fills me as a
  Void

Its starkness
Strips me
  Raw
I cannot hide
Emotions rising from my
  Soul.

With salty eyes
We find the names of
  Death
We trace white letters
Fallen heroes, finally lifted
  Up

We weep
But tears are not the
  Same

Tears

You cry
  For those who died
I cry
  Relieved white letters
Do not spell
  Your name.

Love, Honor and What?

$\mathcal{A}$s a young girl I did the best I could
  To obey my parents
Sometimes I missed the mark
  But I tried.

When I decided to marry
  One thing was clear:
I would not make a promise
  To "obey."

How could I take a vow
  To obey anyone?
I didn't want to start my marriage
  With a promise I wouldn't keep.

Love,
Honor and
What?

Without question, I promised "To Love"
   I will never break faith on that.
I gladly agreed "To Honor"
   Keeping that promise has been easy.

But obey?
   On what issues?
   How often?
How could someone else think for me?

I did not take a vow "To Obey."

Instead, our ceremony was a beautiful poem
   No one had heard before.
Few people caught the notable omission,
   But I kept my conscience clear.

The problem I have with the word obey
Is that it's easily misunderstood.
   "To obey" does not mean
     "To stop thinking"
   "To obey" does not mean
     "Power over the wife"
although it's misinterpreted that way.

58

I think it's better
  To talk things through—together
  To make decisions—together
Instead of having my husband decide
  While I merely follow his direction.
What happens when he's wrong?

I do listen to him, though.
I value his counsel most
  His observations are fair
  His motives are my best interests.

But listening is different from "obeying"
Because I decide
  When he's right
  When he's wrong.
I make the choice to follow his advice
  Not because I obey
  But because I respect his judgment.

When it comes to vows
I think that "Love, Honor and Cherish"
   Makes more sense.
We BOTH made that same promise
   To each other.

It is a promise I CAN keep.
It is a promise I WILL keep.

Separate but Equal

In law school I studied *Plessy v Ferguson:*
"Separate but equal."

Within the context of law,
I never understood
How "separate but equal"
Could EVER be anything but
  Unequal
It's the separation,
  Especially when it's forced,
That CREATES inequality.

Within the context of my marriage, though,
  Separate but equal makes sense.

Separate identities
Separate careers
Separate analysis
   By equal partners
Has helped us create
   Independence
   Self-reliance
   Self-confidence
   Mutual respect.

Marriage is a balance beam
Ours is strong
   Because the weight is balanced
Not by one domineering pillar
In the middle
   Tending to tip things
   In a controlling, self-centered direction
But by two separate, equal pillars
At both ends
   Tending to prevent
   Any tipping.

I'd rather walk on a beam
    That is balanced
    At both ends
It makes my life
    Predictable
    Rational
    Stable.

Flaws

*T*ruth
Shortest distance
Between two points
Yet
We take so long
To arrive

Vulnerability
Open route
Between two hearts
Too often
The road
Is closed

Constancy
  Enduring bond
  Between two souls
Except
  Weak links
  Can stretch and break

Sincerity
  Genuine conflict
  Resolution
But disguised conditions
  Mask honest compromise

Marriage attributes
  Essential qualities
  Of peaceful living
Disrupted by
  Imponderable flaws
  Of human nature

Marriage Cracks

*E*xcessive strain
  In marriage
Is like metal fatigue
  A weakened structure
  With lost resilience

Fractures
  Producing insidious damage
Cracks
  Destroying stability
  If unrepaired.

Financial worries
　Incessant demands
Create marriage cracks:
　Fused mettle
　Splitting apart.

Thwarted plans
　Unending disappointments
Produce breaks:
　Man and woman joined
　But unconnected.

Acrid disagreements
　Harsh words
Deform minds of steel:
　Two people bent
　By discord.

Hidden agendas
　Silent communication
Distort integrity:
　Husband and wife
　Attached but disengaged.

Marriage Cracks

Metal fatigue
    Inevitable failure
Preventable with
    Diligent care
    Constant maintenance.

Marriage cracks
    Symptomatic gaps
Correctable with
    Improved resilience
    Diminished strain.

Opposites

*R*ushing
To achieve
To accomplish
To attain
I did not ask
Why
For whom
At what cost

Now
An experienced
"Rusher"
I long for
Peace
and
Quiet.

Pushing
  My husband
  Myself
  Our limits
I did not ask
  Why
  For whom
  At what cost

Now
An experienced
  "Pusher"
I search for
  Calm
    and
  Contentment.

Demanding
  Dedication
  Effort
  Results
I did not care
  Why
  For whom
  At what cost

Opposites

Now
An experienced
  "Demander"
I hope for
  Understanding
    and
    Simplicity.

Opposites attract
  Even
  Within
My own
  Soul.

Directions

*W*hen we lived
  In Europe
I thought you wanted me
  To ask directions
Because I knew the language better.
  You had me fooled!

Years later
  No matter where we are
I know why you want me
  To ask directions:
Because you won't.
  I'm no longer fooled!

Betrayal

We stood inside
  The narrow house in Amsterdam
We heard the chimes
  She must have heard that day
We saw her hiding place
  The attic she called home

Anne Frank
Betrayed by those she did not know.

We stood aside
  Brick ovens in Dachau
We heard the guide
  Explain what happened in the camp
We saw the "welcome" sign
  "Arbeit macht frei"

Inhabitants
Betrayed by those they did not know.

We stand beside
  One of our dearest friends
We hear her devastating tale
  Of marriage knifed
We see her anguished face
  Bewildered at her loss

Our friend
Betrayed by him she loved the most.

Holding Patterns

Against heaven's backdrop
  Planes approach the field
Each must land
  On the same runway
  At different times

You are part of
  A holding pattern:
  Pilot in command.

Instructions
  From the tower
Separate you
  From other aircraft

Holding patterns
Keep you distant
  From fellow pilots
Keep you safe
  From close encounters.

Against earth's backdrop
  We approach "our" life
Each must walk
  On different paths
  At the same time

We are part of
  A holding pattern:
  Neither in command.

Instructions
  From our souls
Pull us
  Toward each other

Holding patterns
Keep us near
  Physically, emotionally
Keep us safe
  For close encounters.

Thus Far

*M*oving through the air,
In command,
You fly;
Your second love.

Moving through the house,
In prayer,
I wait
For safe return.

No dreaded phone call.
Only a
Silent ring
Thus far.

Quicksand

Schemers
 Unheralded
Deceivers
 Unknown
Intuition
 Unheeded
Quicksand
 Straight ahead

Investment
 Unwise
Commitment
 Unsound
Belief
 Unjustified
Quicksand
 Draws in

Fear
  Unbounded
Answers
  Unseen
Exit
  Unnoticed
Quicksand
  Pulls down

Promises
  Broken
Lies
  Abound
Truth
  Revealed
Quicksand
  All around

Ability
  Questioned
Confidence
  Gone
Future
  Uncertain
Quicksand
  Crushes us

Seize
  Each other
Cling
  To faith

Quicksand

Plead
  For departure
Quicksand
  Gives way

Sense
  God's presence
Trust
  His power
Feel
  His grasp
Quicksand
  Gives us up

Support
  For each other
Vigor
  Renewed
Lives
  Reestablished
Quicksand
  Left behind

Changes

We thought
  We should map out our future
Change
  Redefines the boundaries

We tried
  To script our careers
Change
  Pushes us in new directions

We charted
  Plans for our marriage
Change
  Forces us off course

Changes

We resolved
  To keep order in our lives
Change
  Upsets our patterns

We hoped
  For peace of mind
Change
  Looms overhead

We have learned

Ignore the direction
  Of change
Regret
  The consequences

Resist the demands
  Of change
Lament
  Inflexibility

Disregard the power
  Of change
Rue
  Its presence

Change
  Our dictatorial
Family member
  Ever present
  Ever relentless

Weavings

My parents gave me
  A small weaving loom
  One Christmas
  Long past
I learned to weave
  Potholders

Sometimes the yarn
  Was loose
  Easy to weave
  But worthless
As a potholder
  Not enough heat protection

Often the yarn
  Was tight
  Hard to weave
  But useful
As a potholder
  Protecting my mother's hands

Marriage is like
  The strands
  Man and woman
  Different strengths
Woven together
  To make a life

Sometimes our efforts
  Are like loose yarn
  Already stretched
  And worthless
As protection
  Against life's cauldrons

Often our efforts
   Are like tight yarn
   Strong and lasting
   Reliable and trustworthy
Dependable protection
   Against life's conductive forces

After decades of practice
   We are learning
   To recognize
   And discard
Loose yarn
   Easy weaving
From our marriage loom

Keepsakes

Grandpa had a basket
  Of mementos
He used to look at
  All the time

  Little things
With great meaning
  Accumulated over ninety years
Were in that basket

  Before his stroke
Grandpa used to read us a letter
  From the President
It was the basket's prize

Keepsakes

Every visit
Every time
Every chance
He showed us his treasures

Our letters
Our pictures
Our postcards
Were not in Grandpa's basket

Not until he went
To the home.

After Grandpa died
Mom told us
About the basket's additions

Grandpa wanted
Our letters
Our pictures
Our postcards
With him at the end

Heartfelt words
    Long since sent
Treasured a lifetime

It took
    So little time
    So little effort
    So little care
For us
    To create emotion
    Sustaining forever

Our marriage has its own treasures
    Locks of hair
    Slides of Montmartre
    Sanibel seashells
    Caribbean coral
    Grandma's fur collar

Most of our keepsakes
    Fit in a basket too

Sparks

y friends say I
   Shamelessly
   Constantly
   Audaciously
Flirt with you

I admit it
I love you.

During times apart I
   Habitually
   Boundlessly
   Endlessly
Miss you

I can't help it
I love you.

If I could choose again
  Easily
  Instantly
  Eternally
I would choose you

I mean it
I love you.

You, Love

Whom can I count on
When I've had a tough day
Who will be there
To send trouble away?
You, Love.

To whom can I turn
When I need good advice
Who will listen
Who has no avarice?
You, Love.

Where do I go
When I've lost my way
When I can't see ahead
When the future is gray?
To You, Love.

Who will sustain me
When I'm sick and afraid
Who will give strength
And administer aid?
You, Love.

Who infrequently looks
At the downside of life
But who frequently says,
"I'm so glad she's my wife"?
You, Love.

Who gives support
Even when hope has died
Who always prods:
"Are you sure you have tried?"
You, Love.

You, Love
Are the One
It has always been so
Empowering each other
We will cope with life's woes.

To Hold

"To hold" means:

Enfolding each other with joy
Whenever it's needed the most

Protecting the one who is down
With a shield of emotional strength

Encircling resolve that is weak
With the power of one who is strong

Correcting the path that is off
By redefining the goals

Uplifting the spirit that sags
With humor and unsinking grit

Restraining words born of ire
When words born of wisdom are scarce

Clasping the body that's sick
Infusing a wellstream of love

Lying in bed, limb to limb
Sharing most intimate thoughts

Embracing life's difficult times
Helping each other survive

Shouldering more than our share
When one of us cannot go on

Clutching the lifeline of love
When it's time to let one of us go

Cherishing memories of joy
If one of us lingers behind.

Each Other

e loved
  But
Our babies
  Were unborn

  Still
We have each other

We planned
  But
Not for
  This

  Even so
We have each other

We dreamed
 But
Dreams aren't
 Real

 Yet
We have each other

Who Could Have Guessed?

I couldn't have guessed
When we were still kids
Marriage would be
Important to me

I could not have believed
If someone had said
I would long for the day
When you share my bed

It's hard to imagine
A more distant thought
Than life with a lover
Something I'd never sought

But who really knows
What life has in store
Unexpected surprises
Are what I hope for

I never thought
My life could be changed
By someone like you
All my goals rearranged

Who could have guessed
It would ever be true
I'd be more in love now
Than when I married you?

*Who Could
Have
Guessed?*

It Isn't You

I said "No"
But not to you
I said "Later"
But love's not through!

Solitude
From time to time
Helps clear my head
Helps free my mind.

You don't believe
It's not rejection
If I say "Wait" . . .
Hold your affection

For just awhile
Until this passes
Until I'm free
From love's distractions

Until my mind
Is fixed on us . . .
But until then
Don't make a fuss.

Love's ego is
A fragile thing—
It breaks apart
Or takes on wings.

How can we know
Its fickle moods?
Is this the night
For solitude?

Or is it time
To be caressed
To be held close
Upon my breast?

Is it the night
That we will share
A rapt'rous flight
Profound and rare?

How can you know
My point of view
My deepest thoughts
My lead, your cue?

To make sure that
My eyes don't glisten
With needless tears
You have to listen

It isn't you!
Don't be intrusive
When I need time . . .
I'm not elusive.

It Isn't You

You know it's true:
I need you near
E'en when my eyes
Are filled with tears.

Our love is sure
I hear its call
Despite missed cues
Your clasp enthralls.

Please don't misread
When I say "No"
It isn't you . . .
We're never foes!

Interludes

*Q*uiet times together are special
Such interludes are necessary for my well-being
Intimate moments, sustaining embraces
  Passionate vulnerability
Help to make my marriage complete.

As a young bride I didn't fully grasp
  The virtues of physical intimacy
I didn't realize sensual closeness contributes
  To emotional fulfillment.

As a woman I value
  The need
  The effects
  The desire.

I finally understand the reasons
  For differing physical responses:

Quickness creates a sense of urgency
  And need for constant reattachment

  While

Slowness creates a deeper meaning
  For each experience.

Both responses are indispensable.

Physical interludes
  When all else stops
Are miracles in their own right.
Each time we create moments of passion
  Our individual lives are enriched.

My logic tells me something
  So powerful
  So uninhibiting
  So mutually satisfying
Didn't "just happen"
Didn't "just evolve"

It had to be fashioned
  By the Creator
Who
  Made it profound
  Gave it as a gift
  Intends for it to bind us together.

Surprised by Joy

Mutual friends
  Thought
You and I should
  Meet
We'd be a team
  They said

  We were
Surprised by love.

I was a
  Child
Unskilled in
  Worldly ways
I would achieve
  You said

I was
Surprised by strength.

My greatest
   Wish
For children just
   Like us
Was not to be
   God said

We were
Surprised by pain.

Financial loss
   Set back
Our hopes and plans
   Success
Is not for us
   We said

We were
Surprised by faith.

Surprised
by Joy

We now are
　　One
Each other's closest
　　Friend
We have the best
　　We say

　　We've been
Surprised by joy.

Moldings

Marriage is a sculptor
  Spouses are the sculptor's medium.
The resulting work
  Is a piece of art.

Occasionally the medium is clay
  Pliable and easily changed.

Often the medium is iron
  Firm and inexorably unyielding.

Rarely the medium is alabaster
  Smooth, with few rough edges.

Moldings

Sometimes the medium is marble
   Solid raw material requiring
   A master's chiseling.

With time, the effects of marriage
   On each spouse
   Change both.

Whether changes work
   Depends on the sculptor's skill
   And the medium at hand:

Clay can be quickly molded
   Without an investment of time or talent

Iron needs to be fired
   But it takes time to bend

Alabaster is beautiful when highly polished
   But it breaks if mishandled

Marble—Michelangelo's exquisite
        medium—
    Requires the skill of an artist's chisel
    But the result is lasting and beautiful.

I like to think that in our marriage
    The sculptor used marble

The result is a work-in-progress
That tends to look better
    And more polished
As each year ends.

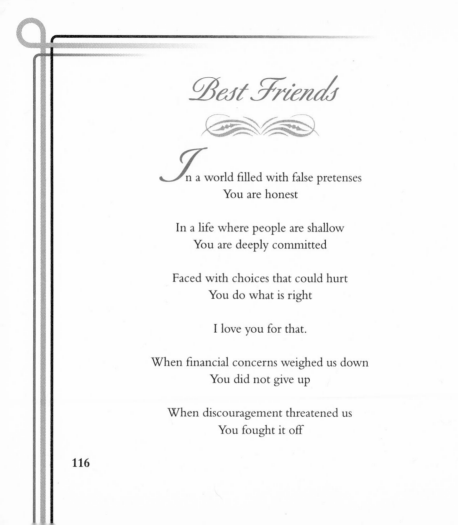

Best Friends

In a world filled with false pretenses
You are honest

In a life where people are shallow
You are deeply committed

Faced with choices that could hurt
You do what is right

I love you for that.

When financial concerns weighed us down
You did not give up

When discouragement threatened us
You fought it off

When our spirits were nearly broken
You stimulated repair

I love you for that.

Your sense of humor brightens my day
You give me hope

Your crazy ideas make me laugh
You expand my life

Your exotic plans make me dream
You have taught me well

I love you for that.

You believe in me when I doubt myself
You help me go on

You encourage me when I'm overwhelmed
You support my career

Best Friends

You stood by me when I was ill
You helped me get well

You are my best friend.
I love you for that.

Our Paradise

*B*odies
Weary from the winter weld of snowfall

Spirits
Chastened by the dearth of sun-filled days

Leave
Behind the nonstop pace of working

Return
To verdant speck of rock amidst the sea

Sunshine
Brilliantly devoid of gray distractions

Fronds
Of palm trees flowing in the breeze

Beach
Commanding me to run each morning

Waves
Turquoise gems crystalline pure

Air
Free from technology's pollution

Flowers
Magenta, purple, yellow, red

People
Whose kindly faces lack the stress of living

Mountain
Spires aloft; goats grazing on the hills

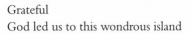

Our Paradise

Grateful
God led us to this wondrous island

Prayerful
We'll return when days at home are bleak

Hopeful
We'll build a house atop the mountain

Mindful
Our working years are not complete

Leave
These pristine shores of paradise till next time

Return
To frozen landscapes, stark and white

Bodies
Recharged and fit to master daily struggles

Spirits
Determined to pursue our dream of island life

Wavelength

You bought Christmas paper
  So did I
Hundreds of choices
  Scores of stores

We each chose
  Two identical rolls
From the same shop
  On the same day

Amazing!

Reflecting on the day's events
  We tell
Each other
  Our stories

*Till Death
Do Us
Part*

With so much uncertainty, crime, and abuse
That exists, everywhere, all around us
More than ever we need to hold fast to the truth
Of our marriage . . . Life will not confound us.

Time together is fleeting; it is too scarce to waste
My goal is to make my life-mission
A beautiful tapestry highlighting "us"
Sewn with threads from our human condition.

I want to explore the full spectrum of life
Before we're too close to its leaving
I want to embrace vast explosions of joy
That make both our hearts strong and heaving.

I know I will love you for all of my life
No matter the time we are given.
I'm yours till death parts us—left all alone—
Until God reunites us in heaven.